Experiments In Government
And
The Essentials Of The Constitution

by

Elihu Root

ABOUT THE AUTHOR

Elihu Root (February 15, 1845 - February 7, 1937) was an American lawyer, Republican politician, and statesman who served as the 41st Secretary of War and 38th Secretary of State under Presidents William McKinley and Theodore Roosevelt. He pioneered the American practice of international law in both posts, as well as over a long legal career. Root is frequently regarded as the model for the twentieth-century political "wise man," advising presidents on a variety of foreign and home matters. He was also a United States Senator from New York and earned the Nobel Peace Prize in 1912.

CONTENTS

PREFACE

The familiar saying that nothing is settled until it is settled right expresses only a half truth. Questions of general and permanent importance are seldom finally settled. A very wise man has said that "short of the multiplication table there is no truth and no fact which must not be proved over again as if it had never been proved, from time to time." Conceptions of social rights and obligations and the institutions based upon them continue unquestioned for long periods as postulates in all discussions upon questions of government. Whatever conduct conforms to them is assumed to be right. Whatever is at variance with them is assumed to be wrong. Then a time comes when, with apparent suddenness, the ground of discussion shifts and the postulates are denied. They cease to be accepted without proof and the whole controversy in which they were originally established is fought over again.

The people of the United States appear now to have entered upon such a period of re-examination of their system of government. Not only are political parties denouncing old abuses and demanding new laws, but essential principles embodied in the Federal Constitution of 1787, and long followed in the constitutions of all the states, are questioned and denied. The wisdom of the founders of the Republic is disputed and the political ideas which they repudiated are urged for approval.

I wish in these lectures to present some observations which may have a useful application in the course of this process.

I
EXPERIMENTS

There are two separate processes going on among the civilized nations at the present time. One is an assault by socialism against the individualism which underlies the social system of western civilization. The other is an assault against existing institutions upon the ground that they do not adequately protect and develop the existing social order. It is of this latter process in our own country that I wish to speak, and I assume an agreement, that the right of individual liberty and the inseparable right of private property which lie at the foundation of our modern civilization ought to be maintained.

The conditions of life in America have changed very much since the Constitution of the United States was adopted. In 1787 each state entering into the Federal Union had preserved the separate organic life of the original colony. Each had its center of social and business and political life. Each was separated from the others by the barriers of slow and difficult communication. In a vast territory, without railroads or steamships or telegraph or telephone, each community lived within itself.

Now, there has been a general social and industrial rearrangement. Production and commerce pay no attention to state lines. The life of the country is no longer grouped about state capitals, but about the great centers of continental production and trade. The organic growth which must ultimately determine the form of institutions has been away from the mere union of states towards the union of individuals in the relation of national citizenship.

The same causes have greatly reduced the independence of personal and family life. In the eighteenth century life was simple. The producer and consumer were near together and could find each other. Every one who had an equivalent to give in property or service could readily secure the support of himself and his family without asking anything from government except the preservation of order. To-day almost all Americans are dependent upon the action of a great number of other persons mostly unknown. About half of our people are crowded into the cities and large towns. Their food, clothes, fuel, light, water—all come from distant sources, of which they are in the main ignorant, through a vast, complicated machinery of production and distribution with which they have little direct relation. If anything occurs to interfere with the working of the machinery, the consumer is individually helpless. To be certain that he and his family may continue to live he must seek the power of combination with others, and in the end he inevitably calls upon that great combination of all citizens which we call government to do something more than merely keep the peace—to regulate the machinery of production and distribution and safeguard it from interference so that it shall continue to work.

A similar change has taken place in the conditions under which a great part of our people engage in the industries by which they get their living. Under comparatively simple industrial conditions the relation between employer and employee was mainly a relation of individual to individual, with individual freedom of contract and freedom of opportunity essential to equality in the commerce of life. Now, in the great manufacturing, mining, and transportation industries of the country, instead of the free give and take of individual contract there is substituted a vast system of collective bargaining between great masses of men organized and acting through their representatives, or the individual on the one side accepts what he can get from superior power on the other. In the movement of these mighty forces of organization the individual laborer, the individual stockholder, the individual consumer, is helpless.

There has been another change of conditions through the development of political organization. The theory of political activity which had its origin approximately in the administration of President Jackson, and which is characterized by Marcy's declaration that "to the victors belong the spoils," tended to make the possession of office the primary and all-absorbing purpose of political conflict. A complicated system of party organization and representation grew up under which a disciplined body of party workers in each state supported each other, controlled the machinery of nomination, and thus controlled nominations. The members of state legislatures and other officers, when elected, felt a more acute responsibility to the organization which could control their renomination than to the electors, and therefore became accustomed to shape their conduct according to the wishes of the nominating organization. Accordingly the real power of government came to be vested to a high degree in these unofficial political organizations, and where there was a strong man at the head of an organization his control came to be something very closely approaching dictatorship. Another feature of this system aggravated its evils. As population grew, political campaigns became more expensive. At the same time, as wealth grew, corporations for production and transportation increased in capital and extent of operations and became more dependent upon the protection or toleration of government. They found a ready means to secure this by contributing heavily to the campaign funds of political organizations, and therefore their influence played a large part in determining who should be nominated and elected to office. So that in many states political organizations controlled the operations of government, in accordance with the wishes of the managers of the great corporations. Under these circumstances our governmental institutions were not working as they were intended to work, and a desire to break up and get away from this extra constitutional method of controlling our constitutional government has caused a great part of the new political methods of the last few years. It is manifest that the laws which were entirely adequate under the conditions of a century ago to secure individual and public welfare must be in many respects inadequate to accomplish the same results under all these new conditions; and our people are now engaged in the difficult but imperative duty of adapting their laws to the life of to-day. The changes in conditions have come very rapidly and a good deal of experiment will be necessary to find out just what government can do and ought to do to meet them.

The process of devising and trying new laws to meet new conditions naturally leads to the question whether we need not merely to make new laws but also to modify the principles upon which our government is based and the institutions of government designed for the application of those principles to the affairs of life. Upon this question it is of the utmost importance that we proceed with considerate wisdom.

By institutions of government I mean the established rule or order of action through which the sovereign (in our case the sovereign people) attains the ends of government. The governmental institutions of Great Britain have been established by the growth through many centuries of a great body of accepted rules and customs which, taken together, are called the British Constitution. In this country we have set forth in the Declaration of Independence the principles which we consider to lie at the basis of civil society "that all men are created equal; that they are endowed, by their Creator, with certain unalienable rights; that among these are life, liberty, and the pursuit of happiness. That to secure these rights, governments are instituted among men, deriving their just powers from the consent of the governed."

In our Federal and State Constitutions we have established the institutions through which these rights are to be secured. We have declared what officers shall make the laws, what officers shall execute them, what officers shall sit in judgment upon claims of right under them. We have prescribed how these officers shall be selected and the tenure by which they shall hold their offices. We have limited them in the powers which they are to exercise, and, where it has been deemed necessary, we have imposed specific duties upon them. The body of rules thus prescribed constitute the governmental institutions of the United States.

When proposals are made to change these institutions there are certain general considerations which should be observed.

The first consideration is that free government is impossible except through prescribed and established governmental institutions, which work out the ends of government through many separate human agents, each doing his part in obedience to law. Popular will cannot execute itself directly except through a mob. Popular will cannot get itself executed through an irresponsible executive, for that is simple autocracy. An executive limited only by the direct expression of popular will cannot be held to responsibility against his will, because, having possession of all the powers of government, he can prevent any true, free, and general expression adverse to himself, and unless he yields voluntarily he can be overturned only by a revolution. The familiar Spanish-American dictatorships are illustrations of this. A dictator once established by what is or is alleged to be public choice never permits an expression of public will which will displace him, and he goes out only through a new revolution because he alone controls the machinery through which he could be displaced peaceably. A system with a plebiscite at one end and Louis Napoleon at the other could not give France free government; and it was only after the humiliation of defeat in a great war and the horrors of the Commune that the French people were able to establish a government that would really execute their will through carefully devised institutions in which they gave their chief executive very little power indeed.

We should, therefore, reject every proposal which involves the idea that the people can rule merely by voting, or merely by voting and having one man or group of men to execute their will.

A second consideration is that in estimating the value of any system of governmental institutions due regard must be had to the true functions of government and to the limitations imposed by nature upon what it is possible for government to accomplish. We all know of course that we cannot abolish all the evils in this world by statute or by the enforcement of statutes, nor can we prevent the inexorable law of nature which decrees that suffering shall follow vice, and all the evil passions and folly of mankind. Law cannot give to depravity the rewards of virtue, to indolence the rewards of industry, to indifference the rewards of ambition, or to ignorance the rewards of learning. The utmost that government can do is measurably to protect men, not against the wrong they do themselves but against wrong done by others and to promote the long, slow process of educating mind and character to a better knowledge and nobler standards of life and conduct. We know all this, but when we see how much misery there is in the world and instinctively cry out against it, and when we see some things that government may do to mitigate it, we are apt to forget how little after all it is possible for any government to do, and to hold the particular government of the time and place to a standard of responsibility which no government can possibly meet. The chief motive power which has moved mankind along the course of development that we call the progress of civilization has been the sum total of intelligent selfishness in a vast number of individuals, each working for his own support, his own gain, his own betterment. It is that which has cleared the forests and cultivated the fields and built the ships and railroads, made the discoveries and inventions, covered the earth with commerce, softened by intercourse the enmities of nations and races, and made possible the wonders of literature and of art. Gradually, during the long process, selfishness has grown more intelligent, with a broader view of individual benefit from the common good, and gradually the influences of nobler standards of altruism, of justice, and human sympathy have impressed themselves upon the conception of right conduct among civilized men. But the complete control of such motives will be the millennium. Any attempt to enforce a millennial standard now by law must necessarily fail, and any judgment which assumes government's responsibility to enforce such a standard must be an unjust judgment. Indeed, no such standard can ever be forced. It must come, not by superior force, but from the changed nature of man, from his willingness to be altogether just and merciful.

A third consideration is that it is not merely useless but injurious for government to attempt too much. It is manifest that to enable it to deal with the new conditions I have described we must invest government with authority to interfere with the individual conduct of the citizen to a degree hitherto unknown in this country. When government undertakes to give the individual citizen protection by regulating the conduct of others towards him in the field where formerly he protected himself by his freedom of contract, it is limiting the liberty of the citizen whose conduct is regulated and taking a step in the direction of paternal government. While the new conditions of industrial life make it plainly necessary that many such steps shall be taken, they should be taken only so far as they are necessary and are effective. Interference with individual liberty by government should be jealously watched and restrained, because the habit of undue interference destroys that independence of character without which in its citizens no free government can endure.

We should not forget that while institutions receive their form from national character they have a powerful reflex influence upon that character. Just so far as a nation allows its institutions to be moulded by its weaknesses of character rather than by its strength it creates an influence to increase weakness at the expense of strength.

The habit of undue interference by government in private affairs breeds the habit of undue reliance upon government in private affairs at the expense of individual initiative, energy, enterprise, courage, independent manhood.

The strength of self-government and the motive power of progress must be found in the characters of the individual citizens who make up a nation. Weaken individual character among a people by comfortable reliance upon paternal government and a nation soon becomes incapable of free self-government and fit only to be governed: the higher and nobler qualities of national life that make for ideals and effort and achievement become atrophied and the nation is decadent.

A fourth consideration is that in the nature of things all government must be imperfect because men are imperfect. Every system has its shortcomings and inconveniences; and these are seen and felt as they exist in the system under which we live, while the shortcomings and inconveniences of other systems are forgotten or ignored.

It is not unusual to see governmental methods reformed and after a time, long enough to forget the evils that caused the change, to have a new movement for a reform which consists in changing back to substantially the same old methods that were cast out by the first reform.

The recognition of shortcomings or inconveniences in government is not by itself sufficient to warrant a change of system. There should be also an effort to estimate and compare the shortcomings and inconveniences of the system to be substituted, for although they may be different they will certainly exist.

A fifth consideration is that whatever changes in government are to be made, we should follow the method which undertakes as one of its cardinal points to hold fast that which is good. Francis Lieber, whose affection for the country of his birth equalled his loyalty to the country of his adoption, once said:

> "There is this difference between the English, French, and Germans: that the English only change what is necessary and as far as it is necessary; the French plunge into all sorts of novelties by whole masses, get into a chaos, see that they are fools and retrace their steps as quickly, with a high degree

of practical sense in all this impracticability; the Germans attempt no change without first recurring to first principles and metaphysics beyond them, systematizing the smallest details in their minds; and when at last they mean to apply all their meditation, opportunity, with its wide and swift wings of a gull, is gone."

This was written more than sixty years ago before the present French Republic and the present German Empire, and Lieber would doubtless have modified his conclusions in view of those great achievements in government if he were writing to-day. But he does correctly indicate the differences of method and the dangers avoided by the practical course which he ascribes to the English, and in accordance with which the great structure of British and American liberty has been built up generation after generation and century after century. Through all the seven hundred years since Magna Charta we have been shaping, adjusting, adapting our system to the new conditions of life as they have arisen, but we have always held on to everything essentially good that we have ever had in the system. We have never undertaken to begin over again and build up a new system under the idea that we could do it better. We have never let go of Magna Charta or the Bill of Rights or the Declaration of Independence or the Constitution. When we take account of all that governments have sought to do and have failed to do in this selfish and sinful world, we find that as a rule the application of new theories of government, though devised by the most brilliant constructive genius, have availed but little to preserve the people of any considerable regions of the earth for any long periods from the evils of despotism on the one hand or of anarchy on the other, or to raise any considerable portion of the mass of mankind above the hard conditions of oppression and misery. And we find that our system of government which has been built up in this practical way through so many centuries, and the whole history of which is potent in the provisions of our Constitution, has done more to preserve liberty, justice, security, and freedom of opportunity for many people for a long period and over a great portion of the earth, than any other system of government ever devised by man. Human nature does not change very much. The forces of evil are hard to control now as they always have been. It is easy to fail and hard to succeed in reconciling liberty and order. In dealing with this most successful body of governmental institutions the question should not be what sort of government do you or I think we should have. What you and I think on such a subject is of very little value indeed. The question should be:

How can we adapt our laws and the workings of our government to the new conditions which confront us without sacrificing any essential element of this system of government which has so nobly stood the test of time and without abandoning the political principles which have inspired the growth of its institutions? For there are political principles, and nothing can be more fatal to self-government than to lose sight of them under the influence of apparent expediency.

In attempting to answer this question we need not trouble ourselves very much about the multitude of excited controversies which have arisen over new methods of extra constitutional-political organization and procedure. Direct nominations, party enrollments, instructions to delegates, presidential preference primaries, independent nominations, all relate to forms of voluntary action outside the proper field of governmental institutions. All these new political methods are the result of efforts of the rank and file of voluntary parties to avoid being controlled by the agents of their own party organization, and to get away from real evils in the form of undue control by organized minorities with the support of organized capital. None of these expedients is an end in itself. They are tentative, experimental. They are movements not towards something definite but away from something definite. They may be inconvenient or distasteful to some of us, but no one need be seriously disturbed by the idea that they threaten our system of government. If they work well they will be an advantage. If they work badly they will be abandoned and some other expedient will be tried, and the ultimate outcome will doubtless be an improvement upon the old methods.

There is another class of new methods which do relate to the structure of government and which call for more serious consideration here. Chief in this class are:

The Initiative; that is to say, direct legislation by vote of the people upon laws proposed by a specified number or proportion of the electors.

The Compulsory Referendum; that is to say, a requirement that under certain conditions laws that have been agreed upon by a legislative body shall be referred to a popular vote and become operative only upon receiving a majority vote.

The Recall of Officers before the expiration of the terms for which they have been elected by a vote of the electors to be had upon the demand of a specified number or proportion of them.

The Popular Review of Judicial Decisions upon constitutional questions; that is to say, a provision, under which, when a court of last resort has decided that a particular law is invalid, because in conflict with a constitutional provision, the law may nevertheless be made valid by a popular vote.

Some of these methods have been made a part of the constitutional system of a considerable number of our states. They have been accompanied invariably by provisions for very short and easy changes of state constitutions, and, so long as they are confined to the particular states which have chosen to adopt them, they may be regarded as experiments which we may watch with interest, whatever may be our opinions as to the outcome, and with the expectation that if they do not work well they also will be abandoned. This is especially true because, since the adoption of the Fourteenth Amendment to the Constitution, the states are prohibited from violating in their own affairs the most important principles of the National Constitution. It is not to be expected, however, that new methods and rules of action in government shall become universal in the states and not ultimately bring about a change in the national system. It will be useful, therefore, to consider whether these new methods if carried into the national system would sacrifice any of the essentials of that system which ought to be preserved.

The Constitution of the United States deals in the main with essentials. There are some non-essential directions such as those relating to the methods of election and of legislation, but in the main it sets forth the foundations of government in clear, simple, concise terms. It is for this reason that it has stood the test of more than a century with but slight amendment, while the modern state constitutions, into which a multitude of ordinary statutory provisions are crowded, have to be changed from year to year. The peculiar and essential qualities of the government established by the Constitution are:

First, it is representative.

Second, it recognizes the liberty of the individual citizen as distinguished from the total mass of citizens, and it protects that liberty by specific limitations upon the power of government.

Third, it distributes the legislative, executive and judicial powers, which make up the sum total of all government, into three separate departments, and specifically limits the powers of the officers in each department.

Fourth, it superimposes upon a federation of state governments, a national government with sovereignty acting directly not merely upon the states, but upon the citizens of each state, within a line of limitation drawn between the powers of the national government and the powers of the state governments.

Fifth, it makes observance of its limitations requisite to the validity of laws, whether passed by the nation or by the states, to be judged by the courts of law in each concrete case as it arises.

Every one of these five characteristics of the government established by the Constitution was a distinct advance beyond the ancient attempts at popular government, and the elimination of any one of them would be a retrograde movement and a reversion to a former and discarded type of government. In each case it would be the abandonment of a distinctive feature of government which has succeeded, in order to go back and try again the methods of government which have failed. Of course we ought not to take such a backward step except under the pressure of inevitable necessity.

The first two of the characteristics which I have enumerated, those which embrace the conception of representative government and the conception of individual liberty, were the products of the long process of development of freedom in England and America. They were not invented by the makers of the Constitution. They have been called inventions of the Anglo-Saxon race. They are the chief contributions of that race to the political development of civilization.

The expedient of representation first found its beginning in the Saxon witenagemot. It was lost in the Norman conquest. It was restored step by step, through the centuries in which parliament established its power as an institution through the granting or withholding of aids and taxes for the king's use. It was brought to America by the English colonists. It was the practice of the colonies which formed the Federal Union. It entered into the constitution as a matter of course, because it was the method by which modern liberty had been steadily growing stronger and broader for six centuries as opposed to the direct, unrepresentative method of government in which the Greek and Roman and Italian republics had failed. This representative system has in its turn impressed itself upon the nations which derived their political ideas from Rome and has afforded the method through which popular liberty has been winning forward in its struggle against royal and aristocratic power and privilege the world over. Bluntschli, the great Heidelberg publicist of the last century, says:

> "Representative government and self-government are the great works of the English and American peoples. The English have produced representative monarchy with parliamentary legislation and parliamentary government.

The Americans have produced the representative republic. We Europeans upon the Continent recognize in our turn that in representative government alone lies the hoped-for union between civil order and popular liberty."

The Initiative and Compulsory Referendum are attempts to cure the evils which have developed in our practice of representative government by means of a return to the old, unsuccessful, and discarded method of direct legislation and by rehabilitating one of the most impracticable of Rousseau's theories. Every candid student of our governmental affairs must agree that the evils to be cured have been real and that the motive which has prompted the proposal of the Initiative and Referendum is commendable. I do not think that these expedients will prove wise or successful ways of curing these evils for reasons which I will presently indicate; but it is not necessary to assume that their trial will be destructive of our system of government. They do not aim to destroy representative government, but to modify and control it, and were it not that the effect of these particular methods is likely to go beyond the intention of their advocates they would not interfere seriously with representative government except in so far as they might ultimately prove to be successful expedients. If they did not work satisfactorily they would be abandoned, leaving representative government still in full force and effectiveness.

There is now a limited use of the Referendum upon certain comparatively simple questions. No one has ever successfully controverted the view expressed by Burke in his letter to the electors of Bristol, that his constituents were entitled not merely to his vote but to his judgment, even though they might not agree with it. But there are some questions upon which the determining fact must be the preference of the people of the country or of a community; such as the question where a capital city or a county seat shall be located; the question whether a debt shall be incurred that will be a lien on their property for a specific purpose; the question whether the sale of intoxicating liquors shall he permitted. Upon certain great simple questions which are susceptible of a *yes* or *no* answer it is appropriate that the people should be called upon to express their wish by a vote just as they express their choice of the persons who shall exercise the powers of government by a vote. This, however, is very different from undertaking to have the ordinary powers of legislation exercised at the ballot box.

In this field the weakness, both of the Initiative and of the Compulsory Referendum, is that they are based upon a radical error as to what constitutes the true difficulty of wise legislation. The difficulty is not to determine what ought to be accomplished but to determine how to accomplish it. The affairs with which statutes have to deal as a rule involve the working of a great number and variety of motives incident to human nature, and the working of those motives depends upon complicated and often obscure facts of production, trade, social life, with which men generally are not familiar and which require study and investigation to understand. Thrusting a rigid prohibition or command into the operation of these forces is apt to produce quite unexpected and unintended results. Moreover, we already have a great body of laws, both statutory and customary, and a great body of judicial decisions as to the meaning and effect of existing laws. The result of adding a new law to this existing body of laws is that we get, not the simple consequence which the words, taken by themselves, would seem to require, but a resultant of forces from the new law taken in connection with all existing laws. A very large part of the litigation, injustice, dissatisfaction, and contempt for law which we deplore, results from ignorant and inconsiderate legislation with perfectly good intentions. The only safeguard against such evils and the only method by which intelligent legislation can be reached is the method of full discussion, comparison of views, modification and amendment of proposed legislation in the light of discussion and the contribution and conflict of many minds. This process can be had only through the procedure of representative legislative bodies. Representative government is something more than a device to enable the people to have their say when they are too numerous to get together and say it. It is something more than the employment of experts in legislation. Through legislative procedure a different kind of treatment for legislative questions is secured by concentration of responsibility, by discussion, and by opportunity to meet objection with amendment. For this reason the attempt to legislate by calling upon the people by popular vote to say yes or no to complicated statutes must prove unsatisfactory and on the whole injurious. In ordinary cases the voters will not and cannot possibly bring to the consideration of proposed statutes the time, attention, and knowledge required to determine whether such statutes will accomplish what they are intended to accomplish; and the vote usually will turn upon the avowed intention of such proposals rather than upon their adequacy to give effect to the intention.

This would be true if only one statute were to be considered at one election; but such simplicity is not practicable. There always will be, and if the direct system is to amount to anything there must be, many proposals urged upon the voters at each opportunity.

The measures, submitted at one time in some of the Western States now fill considerable volumes.

With each proposal the voter's task becomes more complicated and difficult.

Yet our ballots are already too complicated. The great blanket sheets with scores of officers and hundreds of names to be marked are quite beyond the intelligent action in detail of nine men out of ten.

The most thoughtful reformers are already urging that the voter's task be made more simple by giving him fewer things to consider and act upon at the same time.

This is the substance of what is called the "Short Ballot" reform; and it is right, for the more questions divide public attention the fewer questions the voters really decide for themselves on their own judgment and the greater the power of the professional politician.

There is moreover a serious danger to be apprehended from the attempt at legislation by the Initiative and Compulsory Referendum, arising from its probable effect on the character of representative bodies. These expedients result from distrust of legislatures. They are based on the assertion that the people are not faithfully represented in their legislative bodies, but are misrepresented. The same distrust has led to the encumbering of modern state constitutions by a great variety of minute limitations upon legislative power. Many of these constitutions, instead of being simple frameworks of government, are bulky and detailed statutes legislating upon subjects which the people are unwilling to trust the legislature to deal with. So between the new constitutions, which exclude the legislatures from power, and the Referendum, by which the people overrule what they do, and the Initiative, by which the people legislate in their place, the legislative representatives who were formerly honored, are hampered, shorn of power, relieved of responsibility, discredited, and treated as unworthy of confidence. The unfortunate effect of such treatment upon the character of legislatures and the kind of men who will he willing to serve in them can well be imagined. It is the influence of such treatment that threatens representative institutions in our country. Granting that there have been evils in our legislative system which ought to be cured, I cannot think that this is the right way to cure them. It would seem that the true way is for the people of the country to address themselves to the better performance of their own duty in selecting their legislative representatives and in holding those representatives to strict responsibility for their action. The system of direct nominations, which is easy of application in the simple proceeding of selecting members of a legislature, and the Short Ballot reform aim at accomplishing that result. I think that along these lines the true remedy is to be found. No system of self-government will continue successful unless the voters have sufficient public spirit to perform their own duty at the polls, and the attempt to reform government by escaping from the duty of selecting honest and capable representatives, under the idea that the same voters who fail to perform that duty will faithfully perform the far more onerous and difficult duty of legislation, seems an exhibition of weakness rather than of progress.

II
ESSENTIALS

In the first of these lectures I specified certain essential characteristics of our system of government, and discussed the preservation of the first—its representative character. The four other characteristics specified have one feature in common. They all aim to preserve rights by limiting power.

Of these the most fundamental is the preservation in our Constitution of the Anglo-Saxon idea of individual liberty. The republics of Greece and Rome had no such conception. All political ideas necessarily concern man as a social animal, as a member of society—a member of the state. The ancient republics, however, put the state first and regarded the individual only as a member of the state. They had in view the public rights of the state in which all its members shared, and the rights of the members as parts of the whole, but they did not think of individuals as having rights independent of the state, or against the state. They never escaped from the attitude towards public and individual civil rights, which was dictated by the original and ever-present necessity of military organization and defense.

The Anglo-Saxon idea, on the other hand, looked first to the individual. In the early days of English history, without theorizing much upon the subject, the Anglo-Saxons began to work out their political institutions along the line expressed in our Declaration of Independence, that the individual citizen has certain inalienable rights—the right to life, to liberty, to the pursuit of happiness, and that government is not the source of these rights, but is the instrument for the preservation and promotion of them. So when a century and a half after the conquest the barons of England set themselves to limit the power of the Crown they did not demand a grant of rights. They asserted the rights of individual freedom and demanded observance of them, and they laid the corner-stone of our system of government in this solemn pledge of the Great Charter:

> "No freeman shall be taken, or imprisoned, or be disseized of his free hold, or his liberties, or his free customs, or be outlawed, or exiled, or otherwise destroyed, but by the lawful judgment of his peers, or by the law of the land."

Again and again in the repeated confirmations of the Great Charter, in the Petition of Rights, in the Habeas Corpus Act, in the Bill of Rights, in the Massachusetts Body of Liberties, in the Virginia Bill of Rights, and, finally, in the immortal Declaration of 1776—in all the great utterances of striving for broader freedom which have marked the development of modern liberty, sounds the same dominant note of insistence upon the inalienable right of individual manhood under government but independent of government, and, if need be, against government, to life and liberty.

It is impossible to overestimate the importance of the consequences which followed from these two distinct and opposed theories of government. The one gave us the dominion, but also the decline and fall of, Rome. It followed the French Declaration of the Rights of Man, with the negation of those rights in the oppression of the Reign of Terror, the despotism of Napoleon, the popular submission to the second empire and the subservience of the individual citizen to official superiority which still prevails so widely on the continent of Europe. The tremendous potency of the other subdued the victorious Normans to the conquered Saxon's conception of justice, rejected the claims of divine right by the Stewarts, established capacity for self-government upon the independence of individual character that knows no superior but the law, and supplied the amazing formative power which has molded, according to the course and practice of the common law, the thought and custom of the hundred millions of men drawn from all lands and all races who inhabit this continent north of the Rio Grande.

The mere declaration of a principle, however, is of little avail unless it be supported by practical and specific rules of conduct through which the principle shall receive effect. So Magna Charta imposed specific limitations upon royal authority to the end that individual liberty might be preserved, and so to the same end our Declaration of Independence was followed by those great rules of right conduct which we call the limitations of the constitution. Magna Charta imposed its limitations upon the kings of England and all their officers and agents. Our constitution imposed its limitations upon the sovereign people and all their officers and agents, excluding all the agencies of popular government from authority to do the particular things which would destroy or impair the declared inalienable right of the individual.

Thus the constitution provides: No law shall be made by Congress prohibiting the free exercise of religion, or abridging the freedom of speech or of the press. The right of the people to keep and bear arms shall not be infringed. The right of the people to be secure in their persons, houses, papers and effects, against unreasonable searches and seizures, shall not be violated. No person shall be subject for the same offense to be twice put in jeopardy of life or limb; nor be compelled, in any criminal case, to be a witness against himself; nor be deprived of life, liberty, or property without due process of law; nor shall private property be taken for public use without just compensation. In all criminal prosecutions, the accused shall enjoy the right to a speedy and public trial, by an impartial jury of the state and district wherein the crime shall have been committed; and to be informed of the nature and cause of the accusation, to be confronted with the witnesses against him, to have compulsory process for obtaining witnesses in his favor, and to have the assistance of counsel for his defense. Excessive bail shall not he required, nor excessive fines imposed, nor cruel and unusual punishment inflicted. The privilege of the writ of habeas corpus shall not be suspended, except in case of rebellion or invasion. No bill of attainder or ex post facto law shall be passed. And by the Fourteenth Amendment, no state shall deprive any person of life, liberty, or property, without due process of law; nor deny to any person within its jurisdiction the equal protection of the law.

We have lived so long under the protection of these rules that most of us have forgotten their importance. They have been unquestioned in America so long that most of us have forgotten the reasons for them. But if we lose them we shall learn the reasons by hard experience. And we are in some danger of losing them, not all at once but gradually, by indifference.

As Professor Sohm says: "The greatest and most far reaching revolutions in history are not consciously observed at the time of their occurrence."

Every one of these provisions has a history. Every one stops a way through which the overwhelming power of government has oppressed the weak individual citizen, and may do so again if the way be opened. Such provisions as these are not mere commands. They withhold power. The instant any officer, of whatever kind or grade, transgresses them he ceases to act as an officer. The power of sovereignty no longer supports him. The majesty of the law no longer gives him authority. The shield of the law no longer protects him. He becomes a trespasser, a despoiler, a law breaker, and all the machinery of the law may be set in motion for his restraint or punishment. It is true that the people who have made these rules may repeal them. As restraints upon the people themselves they are but self-denying ordinances which the people may revoke, but the supreme test of capacity for popular self-government is the possession of that power of self-restraint through which a people can subject its own conduct to the control of declared principles of action.

These rules of constitutional limitation differ from ordinary statutes in this, that these rules are made impersonally, abstractly, dispassionately, impartially, as the people's expression of what they believe to be right and necessary for the preservation of their idea of liberty and justice. The process of amendment is so guarded by the constitution itself as to require the lapse of time and opportunity for deliberation and consideration and the passing away of disturbing influences which may be caused by special exigencies or excitements, before any change can be made. On the contrary, ordinary acts of legislation are subject to the considerations of expediency for the attainment of the particular objects of the moment, to selfish interests, momentary impulses, passions, prejudices, temptations. If there be no general rules which control particular action, general principles are obscured or set aside by the desires and impulses of the occasion. Our knowledge of the weakness of human nature and countless illustrations from the history of legislation in our own country point equally to the conclusion that if governmental authority is to be controlled by rules of action, it cannot be relied upon to impose those rules upon itself at the time of action, but must have them prescribed beforehand.

The second class of limitations upon official power provided in our constitution prescribe and maintain the distribution of power to the different departments of government and the limitations upon the officers invested with authority in each department. This distribution follows the natural and logical lines of the distinction between the different kinds of power—legislative, executive, and judicial. But the precise allotment of power and lines of distinction are not so important as it is that there shall be distribution, and that each officer shall be limited in accordance with that distribution, for without such limitations there can be no security for liberty. If, whatever great officer of state happens to be the most forceful, skillful, and ambitious, is permitted to overrun and absorb to himself the powers of all other officers and to control their action, there ensues that concentration of power which destroys the working of free institutions, enables the holder to continue himself in power, and leaves no opportunity to the people for a change except through a revolution. Numerous instances of this very process are furnished by the history of some of the Spanish-American republics. It is of little consequence that the officer who usurps the power of others may design only to advance the public interest and to govern well. The system which permits an honest and well-meaning man to do this will afford equal opportunity for selfish ambition to usurp power in its own interest. Unlimited official power concentrated in one person is despotism, and it is only by carefully observed and jealously maintained limitations upon the power of every public officer that the workings of free institutions can be continued.

The rigid limitation of official power is necessary not only to prevent the deprivation of substantial rights by acts of oppression, but to maintain that equality of political condition which is so important for the independence of individual character among the people of the country. When an officer has authority over us only to enforce certain specific laws at particular times and places, and has no authority regarding anything else, we pay deference to the law which he represents, but the personal relation is one of equality. Give to that officer, however, unlimited power, or power which we do not know to be limited, and the relation at once becomes that of an inferior to a superior. The inevitable result of such a relation long continued is to deprive the people of the country of the individual habit of independence. This may be observed in many of the countries of Continental Europe, where official persons are treated with the kind of deference, and exercise the kind of authority, which are appropriate only to the relations between superior and inferior.

So the Massachusetts Constitution of 1780, after limiting the powers of each department to its own field, declares that this is done "to the end it may be a government of laws and not of men."

The third class of limitations I have mentioned are those made necessary by the novel system which I have described as superimposing upon a federation of state governments, a national government acting directly upon the individual citizens of the states. This expedient was wholly unknown before the adoption of our constitution. All the confederations which had been attempted before that time were simply leagues of states, and whatever central authority there was derived its authority from and had its relations with the states as separate bodies politic. This was so of the old confederation. Each citizen owed his allegiance to his own state and each state had its obligations to the confederation. Under our constitutional system in every part of the territory of every state there are two sovereigns, and every citizen owes allegiance to both sovereigns—to his state and to his nation. In regard to some matters, which may generally be described as local, the state is supreme. In regard to other matters, which may generally be described as national, the nation is supreme. It is plain that to maintain the line between these two sovereignties operating in the same territory and upon the same citizens is a matter of no little difficulty and delicacy. Nothing has involved more constant discussion in our political history than questions of conflict between these two powers, and we fought the great Civil War to determine the question whether in case of conflict the allegiance to the state or the allegiance to the nation was of superior obligation. We should observe that the Civil War arose because the constitution did not draw a clear line between the national and state powers regarding slavery. It is of very great importance that both of these authorities, state and national, shall be preserved together and that the limitations which keep each within its proper province shall be maintained. If the power of the states were to override the power of the nation we should ultimately cease to have a nation and become only a body of really separate, although confederated, state sovereignties continually forced apart by diverse interests and ultimately quarreling with each other and separating altogether. On the other hand, if the power of the nation were to override that of the states and usurp their functions we should have this vast country, with its great population, inhabiting widely separated regions, differing in climate, in production, in industrial and social interests and ideas, governed in all its local affairs by one all-powerful, central government at Washington, imposing upon the home life and behavior of each community the opinions and ideas of propriety of distant majorities. Not only would this be intolerable and alien to the idea of free self-government, but it would be beyond the power of a central government to do directly. Decentralization would be made necessary by the mass of government business to be transacted, and so our separate localities would come to be governed by delegated authority—by proconsuls authorized from Washington to execute the will of the great majority of the whole people. No one can doubt that this also would lead by its different route to the separation of our Union. Preservation of our dual system of government, carefully restrained in each of its parts by the limitations of the constitution, has made possible our growth in local self-government and national power in the past, and, so far as we can see, it is essential to the continuance of that government in the future.

All of these three classes of constitutional limitations are therefore necessary to the perpetuity of our government. I do not wish to be understood as saying that every single limitation is essential. There are some limitations that might be changed and something different substituted. But the system of limitation must be continued if our governmental system is to continue—if we are not to lose the fundamental principles of government upon which our Union is maintained and upon which our race has won the liberty secured by law for which it has stood foremost in the world.

Lincoln covered this subject in one of his comprehensive statements that cannot be quoted too often. He said in the first inaugural:

> "A majority held in restraint by constitutional checks and limitations and always changing easily with deliberate changes of popular opinion and sentiments the only true sovereign of a free people. Whoever rejects it does of necessity fly to anarchy or despotism."

Rules of limitation, however, are useless unless they are enforced. The reason for restraining rules arises from a tendency to do the things prohibited. Otherwise no rule would be needed. Against all practical rules of limitation—all rules limiting official conduct, there is a constant pressure from one side or the other. Honest differences of opinion as to the extent of power, arising from different points of view make this inevitable, to say nothing of those weaknesses and faults of human nature which lead men to press the exercise of power to the utmost under the influence of ambition, of impatience with opposition to their designs, of selfish interest and the arrogance of office. No mere paper rules will restrain these powerful and common forces of human nature.

The agency by which, under our system of government, observance of constitutional limitation is enforced is the judicial power. The constitution provides that "This constitution, and the laws of the United States which shall be made in pursuance thereof, and all treaties made, or which shall be made, under the authority of the United States, shall be the supreme law of the land; and the judges in every state shall be bound thereby, anything in the constitution or laws of any state to the contrary notwithstanding." Under this provision an enactment by Congress not made in pursuance of the constitution, or an enactment of a state contrary to the constitution, is not a law. Such an enactment should strictly have no more legal effect than the resolution of any private debating society. The constitution also provides that the judicial power of the United States shall extend to all cases in law and equity arising under the constitution and laws of the United States. Whenever, therefore, in a case before a Federal court rights are asserted under or against some law which is claimed to violate some limitation of the constitution, the court is obliged to say whether the law does violate the constitution or not, because if it does not violate the constitution the court must give effect to it as law, while if it does violate the constitution it is no law at all and the court is not at liberty to give effect to it. The courts do not render decisions like imperial rescripts declaring laws valid or invalid. They merely render judgment on the rights of the litigants in particular cases, and in arriving at their judgment they refuse to give effect to statutes which they find clearly not to be made in pursuance of the constitution and therefore to be no laws at all. Their judgments are technically binding only in the particular case decided, but the knowledge that the court of last resort has reached such a conclusion concerning a statute, and that a similar conclusion would undoubtedly be reached in every case of an attempt to found rights upon the same statute, leads to a general acceptance of the invalidity of the statute.

There is only one alternative to having the courts decide upon the validity of legislative acts, and that is by requiring the courts to treat the opinion of the legislature upon the validity of its statutes, evidenced by their passage, as conclusive. But the effect of this would be that the legislature would not be limited at all except by its own will. All the provisions designed to maintain a government carried on by officers of limited powers, all the distinctions between what is permitted to the national government and what is permitted to the state governments, all the safeguards of the life, liberty and property of the citizen against arbitrary power, would cease to bind Congress, and on the same theory they would cease also to bind the legislatures of the states. Instead of the constitution being superior to the laws the laws would be superior to the constitution, and the essential principles of our government would disappear. More than one hundred years ago, Chief Justice Marshall, in the great case of Marbury *vs*. Madison, set forth the view upon which our government has ever since proceeded. He said:

> "The powers of the legislature are defined and limited; and that those limits may not be mistaken or forgotten, the constitution is written. To what purpose are powers limited, and to what purpose is that limit committed to writing, if these limits may, at any time, be passed by those intended to be restrained? The distinction between a government with limited and unlimited powers is abolished, if those limits do not confine the persons on whom they are imposed, and if acts prohibited and acts allowed are of equal obligation. It is a proposition too plain to be contested, that the constitution controls any legislative act repugnant to it; or that the legislature may alter the constitution by an ordinary act.

> "Between these alternatives, there is no middle ground. The constitution is either a superior, paramount law, unchangeable by ordinary means, or it is on a level with ordinary legislative acts, and, like other acts, is alterable when the legislature shall please to alter it. If the former part of the alternative be true, then a legislative act, contrary to the constitution, is not law: if the latter part be true, then written constitutions are absurd attempts, on the part of the people, to limit a power, in its own nature, inimitable.

> "Certainly, all those who have framed written constitutions contemplate them as forming the fundamental and paramount law of the nation, and consequently, the theory of every such government must be, that an act of the legislature, repugnant to the constitution, is void. This theory is essentially attached to a written constitution, and

is, consequently, to be considered by this court as one of the
fundamental principles of our society."

And of the same opinion was Montesquieu who gave the high authority of the *Esprit des Lois* to the declaration that

> "There is no liberty if the power of judging be not separate from the legislative and executive powers; were it joined with the legislative the life and liberty of the subject would be exposed to arbitrary control."

It is to be observed that the wit of man has not yet devised any better way of reaching a just conclusion as to whether a statute does or does not conflict with a constitutional limitation upon legislative power than the submission of the question to an independent and impartial court. The courts are not parties to the transactions upon which they pass. They are withdrawn by the conditions of their office from participation in business and political affairs out of which litigations arise. Their action is free from the chief dangers which threaten the undue extension of power, because, as Hamilton points out in The Federalist, they are the weakest branch of government: they neither hold the purse, as does the legislature, nor the sword, as does the executive. During all our history they have commanded and deserved the respect and confidence of the people. General acceptance of their conclusions has been the chief agency in preventing here the discord and strife which afflict so many lands, and in preserving peace and order and respect for law.

Indeed in the effort to emasculate representative government to which I have already referred, the people of the experimenting states have greatly increased their reliance upon the courts. Every new constitution with detailed orders to the legislature is a forcible assertion that the people will not trust legislatures to determine the extent of their own powers, but will trust the courts.

Two of the new proposals in government, which have been much discussed, directly relate to this system of constitutional limitations made effective through the judgment of the courts. One is the proposal for the Recall of Judges, and the other for the Popular Review of Decisions, sometimes spoken of as the Recall of Decisions.

Under the first of these proposals, if a specified proportion of the voters are dissatisfied with a judge's decision they are empowered to require that at the next election, or at a special election called for that purpose, the question shall be presented to the electors whether the judge shall be permitted to continue in office or some other specified person shall be substituted in his place. This ordeal differs radically from the popular judgment which a judge is called upon to meet at the end of his term of office, however short that may be, because when his term has expired he is judged upon his general course of conduct while he has been in office and stands or falls upon that as a whole. Under the Recall a judge may be brought to the bar of public judgment immediately upon the rendering of a particular decision which excites public interest and he will be subject to punishment if that decision is unpopular. Judges will naturally be afraid to render unpopular decisions. They will hear and decide cases with a stronger incentive to avoid condemnation themselves than to do justice to the litigant or the accused. Instead of independent and courageous judges we shall have timid and time-serving judges. That highest duty of the judicial power to extend the protection of the law to the weak, the friendless, the unpopular, will in a great measure fail. Indirectly the effect will be to prevent the enforcement of the essential limitations upon official power because the judges will be afraid to declare that there is a violation when the violation is to accomplish some popular object.

The Recall of Decisions aims directly at the same result. Under such an arrangement, if the courts have found a particular law to be a violation of one of the fundamental rules of limitation prescribed in the constitution, and the public feeling of the time is in favor of disregarding that limitation in that case, an election is to be held, and if the people in the election vote that the law shall stand, it is to stand, although it be a violation of the constitution; that is to say, if at any time a majority of the voters of a state (and ultimately the same would be true of the people of the United States) choose not to be bound in any particular case by the rule of right conduct which they have established for themselves, they are not to be bound. This is sometimes spoken of as a Popular Reversal of the Decisions of Courts. That I take to be an incorrect view. The power which would be exercised by the people under such an arrangement would be, not judicial, but legislative. The action would not be a decision that the court was wrong in finding a law unconstitutional, but it would be making a law valid which was invalid before because unconstitutional. In such an election the majority of the voters would make a law where no law had existed before; and they would make that law in violation of the rules of conduct by which the people themselves had solemnly declared they ought to be bound. The exercise of such a power, if it is to exist, cannot be limited to the particular cases which you or I or any man now living may have in mind. It must be general. If it can be exercised at all it can and will be exercised by the majority whenever they wish to exercise it. If it can be employed to make a Workmen's Compensation Act in such terms as to violate the constitution, it can be employed to prohibit the worship of an unpopular religious sect, or to take away the property of an unpopular rich man without compensation, or to prohibit freedom of speech and of the press in opposition to prevailing opinion, or to deprive one accused of crime of a fair trial when he has been condemned already by the newspapers. In every case the question whether the majority shall be bound by those general principles of action which the people have prescribed for themselves will be determined in that case by the will of the majority, and therefore in no case will the majority be bound except by its own will at the time.

The exercise of such a power would strike at the very foundation of our system of government. It would be a reversion to the system of the ancient republics where the state was everything and the individual nothing except as a part of the state, and where liberty perished. It would be a repudiation of the fundamental principle of Anglo-Saxon liberty which we inherit and maintain, for it is the very soul of our political institutions that they protect the individual against the majority. "All men," says the Declaration, "are endowed by their Creator with inalienable rights. Governments are instituted to secure these rights." The rights are not derived from any majority. They are not disposable by any majority. They are superior to all majorities. The weakest minority, the most despised sect, exist by their own right. The most friendless and lonely human being on American soil holds his right to life and liberty and the pursuit of happiness, and all that goes to make them up by title indefeasible against the world, and it is the glory of American self-government that by the limitations of the constitution we have protected that right against even ourselves. That protection cannot be continued and that right cannot be maintained, except by jealously preserving at all times and under all circumstances the rule of principle which is eternal over the will of majorities which shift and pass away.

Democratic absolutism is just as repulsive, and history has shown it to be just as fatal, to the rights of individual manhood as is monarchical absolutism.

But it is not necessary to violate the rules of action which we have established for ourselves in the constitution in order to deal by law with the new conditions of the time, for these rules of action are themselves subject to popular control. If the rules are so stated that they are thought to prevent the doing of something which is not contrary to the principles of liberty but demanded by them, the true remedy is to be found in reconsidering what the rules ought to be and, if need be, in restating them so that they will give more complete effect to the principles they are designed to enforce. If, as I believe, there ought to be in my own state, for example, a Workman's Compensation Act to supersede the present unsatisfactory system of accident litigation, and if the constitution forbids such a law—which I very much doubt—the true remedy is not to cast to the winds all systematic self-restraint and to inaugurate a new system of doing whatever we please whenever we please, unrestrained by declared rules of conduct; but it is to follow the orderly and ordinary method of amending the constitution so that the rule protecting the right to property shall not be so broadly stated as to prevent legislation which the principle underlying the rule demands.

The difference between the proposed practice of overriding the constitution by a vote and amending the constitution is vital. It is the difference between breaking a rule and making a rule; between acting without any rule in a particular case and determining what ought to be the rule of action applicable to all cases.

Our legislatures frequently try to evade constitutional provisions, and doubtless popular majorities seeking specific objects would vote the same way, but set the same people to consider what the fundamental law ought to be, and confront them with the question whether they will abandon in general the principles and the practical rules of conduct according to principles, upon which our government rests, and they will instantly refuse. While their minds are consciously and avowedly addressed to that subject they will stand firm for the general rules that will protect them and their children against oppression and usurpation, and they will change those rules only if need be to make them enforce more perfectly the principles which underlie them.

Communities, like individuals, will declare for what they believe to be just and right; but communities, like individuals, can be led away from their principles step by step under the temptations of specific desires and supposed expediencies until the principles are a dead letter and allegiance to them is a mere sham.

And that is the way in which popular governments lose their vitality and perish.

The Roman consuls derived their power from the people and were responsible to the people; but Rome went on pretending that the emperors and their servants were consuls long after the Praetorians were the only source of power and the only power exercised was that of irresponsible despotism.

A number of countries have copied our constitution coupled with a provision that the constitutional guarantees may be suspended in case of necessity. We are all familiar with the result. The guarantees of liberty and justice and order have been forgotten: the government is dictatorship and the popular will is expressed only by revolution.

Nor, so far as our national system is concerned has there yet appeared any reason to suppose that suitable laws to meet the new conditions cannot be enacted without either overriding or amending the constitution. The liberty of contract and the right of private property which are protected by the limitations of the constitution are held subject to the police power of government to pass and enforce laws for the protection of the public health, public morals, and public safety. The scope and character of the regulations required to accomplish these objects vary as the conditions of life in the country vary. Many interferences with contract and with property which would have been unjustifiable a century ago are demanded by the conditions which exist now and are permissible without violating any constitutional limitation. What will promote these objects the legislative power decides with large discretion, and the courts have no authority to review the exercise of that discretion. It is only when laws are passed under color of the police power and having no real or substantial relation to the purposes for which the power exists, that the courts can refuse to give them effect. By a multitude of judicial decisions in recent years our courts have sustained the exercise of this vast and progressive power in dealing with the new conditions of life under a great variety of circumstances. The principal difficulty in sustaining the exercise of the power has been caused ordinarily by the fact that carelessly or ignorantly drawn statutes either have failed to exhibit the true relation between the regulation proposed and the object sought, or have gone farther than the attainment of the legitimate object justified. A very good illustration of this is to be found in the Federal Employer's Liability Act which was carelessly drawn and passed by Congress in 1906 and was declared unconstitutional by the Supreme Court, but which was carefully drawn and passed by Congress in 1908 and was declared constitutional by the same court.

Insistence upon hasty and violent methods rather than orderly and deliberate methods is really a result of impatience with the slow methods of true progress in popular government. We should probably make little progress were there not in every generation some men who, realizing evils, are eager for reform, impatient of delay, indignant at opposition, and intolerant of the long, slow processes by which the great body of the people may consider new proposals in all their relations, weigh their advantages and disadvantages, discuss their merits, and become educated either to their acceptance or rejection. Yet that is the method of progress in which no step, once taken, needs to be retraced; and it is the only way in which a democracy can avoid destroying its institutions by the impulsive substitution of novel and attractive but impracticable expedients.

The wisest of all the fathers of the Republic has spoken, not for his own day alone but for all generations to come after him, in the solemn admonitions of the Farewell Address. It was to us that Washington spoke when he said:

> "The basis of our political systems is the right of the people to make and to alter their constitutions of government; but the Constitution which at any time exists, till changed by an explicit and authentic act of the whole people, is sacredly obligatory upon all.... Towards the preservation of your government, and the permanency of your present happy state, it is requisite, not only that you steadily discountenance irregular oppositions to its acknowledged authority, but also that you resist with care the spirit of innovation upon its principles, however specious the pretexts. One method of assault may be to effect, in the forms of the Constitution, alterations which will impair the energy of the system, and thus to undermine what cannot be directly overthrown. In all the changes to which you may be invited, remember that time and habit are at least as necessary to fix the true character of governments as of other human institutions; that experience is the surest standard by which to test the real tendency of the existing constitution of a country; that facility in changes, upon the credit of mere hypothesis and opinion, exposes to perpetual changes, from the endless variety of hypothesis and opinion."

While, in the nature of things, each generation must assume the task of adapting the working of its government to new conditions of life as they arise, it would be the folly of ignorant conceit for any generation to assume that it can lightly and easily improve upon the work of the founders in those matters which are, by their nature, of universal application to the permanent relations of men in civil society.

Religion, the philosophy of morals, the teaching of history, the experience of every human life, point to the same conclusion—that in the practical conduct of life the most difficult and the most necessary virtue is self-restraint. It is the first lesson of childhood; it is the quality for which great monarchs are most highly praised; the man who has it not is feared and shunned; it is needed most where power is greatest; it is needed more by men acting in a mass than by individuals, because men in the mass are more irresponsible and difficult of control than individuals. The makers of our constitution, wise and earnest students of history and of life, discerned the great truth that self-restraint is the supreme necessity and the supreme virtue of a democracy. The people of the United States have exercised that virtue by the establishment of rules of right action in what we call the limitations of the constitution, and until this day they have rigidly observed those rules. The general judgment of students of government is that the success and permanency of the American system of government are due to the establishment and observance of such general rules of conduct. Let us change and adapt our laws as the shifting-conditions of the times require, but let us never abandon or weaken this fundamental and essential characteristic of our ordered liberty.